BARNBURNER

Dear Daniel and Julia —
Thank you for celebrating this
book with me! I'm a big fan of
David and was hoping to meet you
when he said his dad was a poet.
I hope you enjoy Barnburner,
as fellow fans of art and of
literature.

All best wishes,
Erin Hoover

BARNBURNER

Erin Hoover

ELIXIR PRESS | DENVER, COLORADO

www.elixirpress.com

Book design by Steven Seighman
Artwork by Seana Carmody
Author photo by Kira Derryberry

Library of Congress Cataloging-in-Publication DataNames: Hoover, Erin, author.Title: Barnburner : poems / Erin Hoover.Description: Denver, Colorado : Elixir Press, [2018] | Includes bibliographical references.Identifiers: LCCN 2017056096 | ISBN 9781932418675 (acid-free paper)Classification: LCC PS3608.O6235 A6 2018 | DDC 811/.6--dc23 LC recordavailable at https://lccn.loc.gov/2017056096

10   9   8   7   6   5   4   3   2   1

For Hester

Contents

Introduction

... I want

*the ending we've earned,   not the sucker
punch, but to stand
                with you
in the path of the wallop.*

—Erin Hoover, "Reading Sappho's Fragments"

Erin Hoover's *Barnburner* is sometimes set in small-town Pennsylvania, where one takes the work one can get—reading scripts in a call center, waiting tables, making coffee for the bosses, among other rote tasks that can be made to feel devoid of purpose and dignity. "We weren't allowed to talk, only script-read, and I thought: *Can't they automate this?*"

Having lived the better part of my life in rural Appalachian and rural Missouri communities, I recognize too well in Hoover's poems the alienation and hopelessness, opioid abuse and its ripple effects, anger turned outward, then anger turned inward, like I recognize a mirror.

As I read these poems, I think about the poetics of anger. I think about righteous anger and indignant anger. I think about the absurdity or futility or hypocrisy of anger when you are living on land genocided from under the feet of others atop mines that turned the creeks in the watershed milk turbid or rust orange or clear as a frack-lit match. I think about how productive anger can be when it galvanizes us to action. And about those angers that just can't be made productive or useful, despite one's best efforts, so turn inward into a terrible, self-destructive pain.

There are occasions where nonviolent conflict resolution is an elegant and miraculously effective answer to fascism's fury. And then there are occasions when a sucker punch from some girl you never would have guessed had it in her is its own exquisite response to one more agent of the hegemonic patriarchy and that late-stage capitalist horse it rode in on.

It is commonly the work of introductions like these to position a writer in relation to their literary forebears, and since Hoover's book is largely set in blue collar small towns and written with a conversationally direct and highly narrative style, we should talk about Robert Frost and the pastoral world he contemplated from the far side of a crumbling stone wall. Though Frost doesn't intend it this way, that kind of golden-leaved dirt road cast in the beatific glow of a setting sun has become a dangerous dream that now seasons a certain kind of overcooked nostalgia until that stew tastes like a bitter, entitled gnaw of gristle.

Frost knew this gristle as well as any of us, but wrote, "Good fences make good neighbors," with the ironic restraint and charmingly mannered double entendre of someone who still has something to lose. But why should a woman like Erin Hoover restrain herself, these poems want to know? Restraint doesn't stop sexual assault like the one in "If You Are Confused About Whether a Girl Can Consent." It doesn't make the self-satisfied, privileged classes, like those in "With Gratitude to Those Who Have Made This Book Possible," any more aware of their entitlement or their forsaken responsibilities. Certainly it doesn't stop a gang of bigots from terrorizing the Arab stockboy in "Recalibration." It is the speaker's courage, interrupting the assault to ask, *Do you really have to do this?* that stops them long enough to turn their danger on her instead.

So why not find out what anger can do? What guileless speech might accomplish in place of politeness and rhetoric? Why not find out what happens when you hold yourself responsible for covering for your boyfriend who tried to rape someone. The speaker does this in "What Is the Sisterhood to Me?" and discovers, "Don't say you know yourself / unless you've stepped outside of it, / seen the shadow you cast / in your own bronze light." And then find out what happens when you hold him responsible for his actions and accept that the woman who fought him off with a fire extinguisher is not and never was *some dumb bitch.* You might discover, as the speaker does, "I never would have guessed, / holding the fire extinguisher, / how nearly weightless it is / in my woman's hands."

What happens when a poet goes full throttle are these poems. They remind me of what Audre Lorde said in "The Uses of Anger: Women Responding to Racism" about the power in women's anger. "[A]nger expressed and translated into action in the service of our vision and our future is a liberating and strengthening act of clarification." Not all of the anger in this book is directed at racism, but intersectionality and privilege are recurring themes, and the anger directed at sexism is deeply rooted in Lorde's theories of anger that leads to insight and the possibility of better and more creative understandings. Hoover has this kind of anger, and she also knows she has power. In her poems she puts both to good use in ways that borrow as much from Lorde's poetics of urgent, engaged speech as they do from Frost's portraits of humble folk life.

The epigraph to this book is a call to burn it all down. "According to an old story, there was once a Dutchman who was so bothered by the rats in his barn that he burned down the barn to get rid of them. Thus a 'barn burner' became one who destroyed all in order to get rid of a nuisance." There is honesty in this epigraph, raw and brutal, like the narrative voices in Hoover's poems. But there's an irony at play here, an irony perhaps borrowing a bit from the ironies of Frost's "Mending Wall": Hoover's poems don't burn down the cruelties of a homogeneous, racist patriarchy. Instead, they make a muse of it. A muse that can be objectified, stripped bare, and put on a pedestal for all to scorn. She fridges that muse so that one speaker of a heroine after another is vaulted by the shock of such violence into a journey of personal discovery. There are mean-spirited, ruthless characters in these poems and, in a kind of reverse Bechdel test, Hoover wipes away their inner lives and never lets them talk to each other about anything except those they have hurt.

Barnburner is not your grandfather's apple orchard. It is the book of your mother calling across the neighborhood in a loud, clear voice, with that wooden spoon tapping impatiently against her hand, "You better come on home now, your time's up!"

Kathryn Nuernberger
January 2018

According to an old story, there was once a Dutchman who was so bothered by the rats in his barn that he burned down the barn to get rid of them. Thus a 'barn burner' became one who destroyed all in order to get rid of a nuisance.

—*Morris Dictionary of Word and Phrase Origins*

I.

The Lovely Voice of Samantha West

I once worked at a call center. We weren't
allowed to talk, only script-read, and
I thought: *Can't they automate this?*
Magazine circulars promised twelve
books for a cent, and seemingly eager to
be fooled, our customers skipped the fine
print, mailed in their pennies, and signed
up to pay for a book a month they swore
they didn't want.

Explaining this con dozens of times every
day as an agent of the company, I still
knew I was human, the sort requiring ham
sandwiches and occasionally to urinate.
And I knew, too, the people whose lives
I interrupted as human—wondered if
dust storms clotted their skies in Topeka
or, hearing the scrape of a pot being lifted
from a stove, what dinner they'd made for
the children who fussed through our call.

I had to clock out to use the toilet and
worked in a windowless, chattering room,
but as Americans, we had fans on our
desks, a tap with all the clean water we
could drink, a vending machine as ever
sold out of Sprite. We had our voices,
trained in American English since birth.

Still, it was all I could do to make the
script into a conversation, to be its human
participant. The call center made me an
expert in my voice's currency, what I could
do with its pitches and pauses, my larynx

flexing around the rarely varied words. It was work. Every three hours on the dot I stood outside in a designated area and burned the high-nicotine cigarettes I'd bought.

More recently, I know why, when the nearly human creature they named Samantha West started calling to give people their health insurance quotes, her voice was programmed to sound reassuringly American. But those who picked up their phones knew something wasn't right.

No distractions could pull them from their interrogations. "Hey are you a robot?" "No I am a real person. Maybe we have a bad connection." "Just say, 'I'm not a robot.' Please." "I'm a real person." And so on—all conversation stuck permanently in the uncanny valley.

And yet there was nothing wrong with the monstrous voice of Samantha West. She seemed to be patterned after Doris Day, sunny and mildly titillating, relentless high rising terminals that turned every speech act into a request for approval. The Doris of *Pillow Talk*, cozy in bed in her ruffled nightgown, flirting on the phone with Rock Hudson before realizing he was the dirtbag on her party line. Doris, whose every indignation was cute.

Are you a robot? Samantha West was not technically a robot. And yet her operators on the other side of the world in India, sitting in front of their computers in a crowded, industrial-lit room, not unlike the one where I worked fifteen years before, understandably paused a beat too long when asked this question. Their good middle-class living depended on the correct response. They searched for the command key that would trigger some version of an acceptable answer:

I am a real person.

Frank Sinatra once said, *Doris is the only person who can hit a note and make you feel it like I do.* But for the people Samantha West called, her voice vibrated in the terrifying space between barely and fully human. It reached into their homes in the middle of the day and threatened the necessary belief that conversations take place between *people.* Not eager to be fooled, people recoiled.

On the day I quit, I remember setting down my headset and pressing the "break" button. Later my boss called me at home. *Is there any way we could have made this better for you?* I'd rarely seen Barb's snowbird pixie cut and chunky sweaters on the calling floor. Her voice on the phone had a human response for me, but I was unable to explain why I left.

Conversion Party

Sometimes I look my mother and father
in their wet faces and don't understand—
if they were good, if they were kind to me,
why my tilted masonry, my facial gears

petrified into a smile? One night I wander
to the river to watch fireworks
for the Fourth, among strollered families
tugging along their children, so many

big and little hands. I'm twenty-one,
I've dropped out of college.
And when I'm tamping my blanket
down over the mud, a girl sits nearby,

offers me a ham sandwich from
her bag. I do everything alone these days,
all social interactions the binary
of tolerating someone, or telling them

to go to hell. If I refuse her sandwich,
I've shut down another's kindness. And when
she invites me to a party tomorrow, if I don't
accept, I've agreed to die alone. So as bombs

burst over us, I say sure, picturing the way
other people who get asked to parties
agree to go, effortless, believing they're
wanted. The next day when I show up

in my shitty car, there's actually a cake
embroidered with curlicue frosting,
a glass etched with tulips thrust into my hand.
At first it seems like a life I'd want,

a hearth decked out with children's photos,
this glowing circle of wholesome,
curious neighbors, all looking at me
as if there were something I had

to give them, some part of me cached
beyond my visible husk of afflictions.
I hide the whiskey I've brought behind
a stout philodendron. They'll never believe

my father was a deacon, my mother taught
Sunday school, God and I are on
a first-name basis. Everyone nods like they've all
taken the same workshop on listening skills

as I confess I haven't run away, I have a job,
if slinging plates at a vegan cafe counts.
I'll eat my apportioned acreage of cake
if it satisfies our bargain, where I pretend

smooth surfaces, an ease I don't feel. Maybe
I belong back at the riverbank, wearing
my nonsensical pain like a chainsaw wound,
oblivious to onlookers. I leave the cake

on top of my friendly host's toilet, frosting
melting to a smear, afraid I'll swallow it all.
In a few months, my job will fire me when
the night's take goes missing; easier

for my manager to believe I'd steal
than that he dropped the deposit bag
behind the utility oven by mistake. When
will anyone ever bet on me,

that I can be trusted? For years, after each
church service, I helped my father
count the collection plate. We'd tip over
the giant brass bowls, and I'd wrap

tubes of quarters, smooth out crumpled
dollar bills, the way he taught me,
as the dust stirred by our Bibles fell
with holy industry. Every coin in its place.

The Evacuation Shadow

Every disaster can be drawn
as a target on a map,
radial circles of streets and farms
round a compass point. Once,

that point was the colossal spun pots
of Three Mile Island, and me,
a child pinned to the evacuation
shadow my parents didn't

have the means to leave. Our yards
watered by clouds so absurdly
normal, our tomatoes grown
brawny, sullen fish hooked

from the river. I imagine someone
pulled my infant body close
as the countryside emptied
with its fear around us. Today,

in the still-standing block
apartments of Ukraine, where
Chernobyl permanently blights
the Soviet breadbasket, pictures

tilt on their walls, curtains
drag from their hooks,
backyards are seeded with dolls
and basketballs decades

flat. Those badlands are different
from Appalachia's weedy
hills where we remained.
In those years I remember playing

in the backyard, press of mating
insects so loud I could
disappear if they wanted me
enough. I began to leave the place

I lived from the day I was
born, when adults believed the air
poison, and the water, believed
in the death drive of nations

and worlds. But everyone
has to live somewhere, so like adults,
we children pretended the cornstalks
could be fine after that, the river

clear to its depths, still good
to swim. No choice but to count
our own bodies as safe to roam
inside, protected in our skin.

Anticonfessional

M. called me every day this week. That
is this poem's most important fact. I say it
first, before I tell you he is a junkie.

We all know not to trust what a junkie says.
But I was going through some small lunacy
over a man and M. was the only friend

to call me on it. He said he had research:
minutes after the head detaches from the body,
brain circuits still flare, so if I laid down

on the tracks I had better be ready. That's
porn, though, so I'll stop. I won't describe
the first time M. shot up, how he made

me do it for him. I'd had five years
of allergy shots, and besides, I knew,
if a man wants something, I'm not the girl

to say he's wrong. *The best way to die,*
M. said, *is always heroin. How many
dead geniuses prove it?* As if we too could

be geniuses. He told me that yesterday
he'd run into Smalls in the parking lot
at Topps' bar, told him I'm on the market.

Bootleg sage who's kept M. in Mind Fuck
and Rat Poison and Body Bag for years,
Smalls said, *She'll be okay. Girls like that*

take care of themselves. Smart men see this,
but the world's loaded with dumb men.
The guy with Smalls, teeth flaying the skin

from a chicken thigh, kingpin who
met me once in a parking lot and cited
the street value for my car's parts, said to M.,

next time I'm in town, I've got a free bag,
just come by the bar. Evidence, M. said,
of my options. M. and I share a past, a snag

of memories locked together like hair
tangled in a drain. I saw, in middle school,
when a gang of boys paid a trampy girl

to sit on M.'s lap, stroke his face and whisper,
Sexy, the boys' payoff the revulsion
she tried to squelch looking into his fat face.

None of us is good at hiding that look.
And he knew me in the years revulsion
was my turn-on, kissing on the rusted asses

of navy-yard ships or in nursery school
broom closets. Have I said enough?
Tonight M. calls me from a strip mall

where I waited with him dozens of times,
talking Foucault or robotics, any subject
besides the tangible fact of our lives, the wait

inversely proportional to the quality
of the eventual shit. He thinks he can save
my life with phone calls, with words.

I tell him: junkies are the only people
worth talking to about love, because junkies
are the only ones who ever felt it. Like

our hometown sinkhole on Front Street
that sucked down parked cars,
implosion we always suspected,

as kids riding past, before it opened.
A place to junk the feelings we had.
The ones we didn't believe, the ones we did.

Girls

The point isn't that so-called ugly girls
get laid on HBO, but their mishaps, that if
the single one is funny, a slew of them looks

downright ambitious. They're the bitches
nobody liked in high school, smudge-eyed
and trussed up in complicated skirts,

queuing outside the club with their amber
vials of blow. Our kind of fucking up is Y,
less Millennial, more perpetual, because

we too called ourselves journalists,
wrote for weeklies nobody read. We too
got swept into green rooms on a glance,

our stupid luck that time a drummer sized up
my platinum, six-foot, Australian friend
and invited us backstage. She ended up

with the frontman singing to her outside,
as on a beery couch, that drummer
droned on about off-beats to me. I was his

dark foil, his siren whinging about desire,
while he likely thought, *She's a little bit fat.*
Even before he pushed his demo like bus fare

into my palm, I knew our hook-up
wouldn't do me any good—my nights then
were transcendent in their flaws.

When my friend pulled him off me to say
she and the singer were leaving, her
what were you thinking draped between us

like garlands at an anti-award ceremony.
In that moment, I wanted to be a woman
who could Take Back Some Night Somewhere,

hang with those bad bitches at Seneca Falls,
but I'd kissed a drummer from Staten Island
for no better reason than he chose me.

Does it get any less complicated
than one passed-over object burying itself
in another? To those who say a show like *Girls*

is the third wave finding itself, who speak
from the absurd position of having been *found*,
I offer this grounded but ahistorical fuck you:

I swear our girlish centers burn white-hot
as surely as nothing burns there. It was last call
five minutes ago. Somebody, turn up the lights.

On Joy as the Subject

In my kitchen, I catch palmettos, long
as an index finger, in jelly jars. I'll admit

their wings, lined with tiny orange hairs,
still surprise me. Christ will never leave you,

says my godly friend, but knowing this—
I do—makes it easier to turn away

from Him. Or is it that I trial the Lord
daily: feats of liquor, overwork, rigorous

pursuit of love in all the wrong
airports? I read in friends' faces my same

stake in annihilation. When M. and I buy
drugs in the lobby of our city's fancy hotel,

in full sight of the bellboy, no one chases us
onto the street, though his red coat hurries

down the hallway to the manager,
and he mouths and points. I often think

if I met Christ in such a corridor, he would
step aside, relishing my eternal

thanklessness. He'd smirk as if to say:
This is what makes you happy? I'll confess,

you help me remember my body
is inhabited. I was cooking for us when

the first bug scuffled onto the tile and,
ready to die, turned on his back. I brought

down a jar, trapped him where he lay.
Under it, how those two vivid wings flared.

Epithalamion

For Nora and Jeremy

My nephew was put to bed
in the next room, and now
he and I lie in our dim capsules.
All day he cried. He did not want
to eat any dinner, or
build towers of blocks, or sing
songs about farm animals,
and I wonder if at night
he contemplates his internal edges,
as I did at his age,

in this house. I want to sneak out
and whisper, *Hey, are you sleeping?*
from the hall, as I once
wished a friend would,
make an apology for how
jagged childhood is,
every moment a completely
new trauma, an earache fashioned
of customized pain. It's years
later, and I haven't escaped

this sense of the world, though
I've felt, on occasion,
the pressure lift.
I have been understood. I grew up
believing kindness was
easy, believing it should be.
Too many times
I asked for just one thing,

and it wasn't done, however
simple. Rarely did I ask anyone

to perform the dangerous
feat of stepping into
another mind, carefully,
as in an unlit house
with strange furniture. Such visitors
quiet the animal mind, leaving
only the human one. We ask
so much of the people we want
to love us. Tonight I don't go
to see if my nephew is awake,

but I feel his thoughts
moiling through the walls.
I'll never tell him
to be brave, but if I love him,
he will be. Parents do this
for us. Friends do.
Hoping that later
when others approach,
we'll feel capable. We'll ask
them to come in.

Barrier Islands

Now and again, you order the steak dinner
for yourself at the mahogany bar in this
Jersey resort town where your grandparents
courted. Here, in the only restaurant open
among the shells of Victorian summer homes,

after Sandy's apocalypse, you want to know
if "steak dinner" still means what you think
it does, sirloin and a side of potatoes. Or did
the hurricane change that, too? Most here
wait on insurance money, the rare window lit,

others gaping as skull's eyes. It's been so long
since you talked to anyone. It's as if disaster
has tuned you differently, into an ascetic
filed sharp enough to need the soft containers
of others. So one night you try talking

to the couple next to you, a toned man
you soon learn is a gym instructor
on the mainland, his frizzy, grinning girlfriend
who works for a bank. As you swipe through
their phone snapshots, their concave roof,

tempested balcony, they say they hate
out-of-towners. Do they mean you?
Your hurricane left you mostly untouched,
your beach cabin roof dinged, a few feet
of carpet to replace, that's all. How uneven

circumstance can be, even to people close
as neighbors. There's a TV show now about
Amish kids, where teens from farm towns

like yours try out being "English"—as if your
coming up boiled down to bad dance music

and abundant jello shots. On the show,
one kid stands in Times Square and says,
I'm a sheep in a pigpen. Now, the bar declines
the couple's credit card while you're off taking
a piss. Returning, you find they've emptied

your purse and gone. You'd left it, wanting
to believe in an idea you read about in school,
gemeinschaft, the community ruled by unified
desire, where we depend on one another.
But theirs is the horror show of individual will,

gesellschaft, each unto their own. It's no use
expecting more of any evening than
to drink our gin, pay the check, and disappear
to our cold rooms. The man had told you
about his first job, as a boy scooping ice cream

at the parlor where decades ago, you begged
for a cone. The woman had offered to buy
your dinner, flashing a wallet of cards she said
she won in a raffle. How nice they were, good
at being nice. How they seemed like friends.

Why Don't You Have Kids?

When my friend S. and her son visit me
to swim, she says that a few days ago,
her husband hurled a mug
                of coffee at her—

The storm that knocked out
half the town's lights had blown
a tree trunk down on the roof of S.'s car,
and her husband was pissed
                she tweeted a picture of it

before their son could climb
from the backseat.
The kid was safe, S. says. *Safe.*
I affirm that her husband is
                a jerk, the *worst.*
My house has power, my freezer churns
to cool the popsicles I offer,
                the six-pack

she's asked me to buy.
Her son won't take a popsicle, pouts
at anything I offer. In the pool, he laughs
too often. Her husband has gone
                wherever men go

to disappear. The boy and I race across
the pool, and S. watches as I dog-paddle
to let him win, as I fake outrage
when he accuses me of not really trying.
That's when she asks:
                Why don't you have kids?

I know how I'm supposed to respond,
like I know how to slice water
cleanly with my arms and legs. I should say
I don't want children, or that I want them,
and put forth a short-term plan.
            Instead I tell her,

some people find each other in the midst
                of other things—
the same city block, the same lunch rush
in the taqueria, comparisons of the same
            Black Flag tattoo,
and others don't. *Like we did*, S. says,
about the husband who called her

a bad mother. Meanwhile two new boys
have joined us in the pool, their mothers
smoking at its edge, and the boys soon fight
with S.'s son because he leaps

inside their circle for the action figure
they toss back and forth. They call him
                a freak, and it's a word
I've heard, too.
I turn to one boy, snot-slug
sliding down his lip, and say,

What are you throwing? Can I see it?
Then I catch his throw expertly
because that's important with boys.
                I toss the toy
to S.'s son, who makes a show

of plunging for it. In the changing room,
S. is asking Facebook for an attorney to call,
so it's just me and her son,
            and it's okay.
We play in the piss-warm water,
we dive toward the blur of the toy.

I'm certain, when doctors open
                my corpse,
they'll find this story in all its versions.
With forceps, they'll pull apart
the question women are asked, press
the strands of my answers onto slides.
But this is
            the wrong way to look,

as if all possible offspring
existed in a woman's atmosphere,
as if it were as easy as plucking her child
                from the air.

Reading Sappho's Fragments

I prefer the whole.
                    Despite all the theory I've read,
                              I believe in an understory
nested in what we say to each other, clamoring for air
              beneath. I like the effort
in completion. I am always lifting the banner
                    of a manifesto and
          carrying its shield, like a girl saint
                    in men's armor
                              turning back a siege.

              I do this with words knowing at best
they are a surface,
                              a roof or a cloak
          or hard stitching of a quilt.
                                        But at least I can know,
I am this twist-tie   of wiry nerves
                              sheathed in some thinning
performance of skin.
                    Every day, now, more people are dying
          from cheeseburgers and chokeholds,
                    and I have lived through
so many wars about
                    what people won't say.

    This isn't Sappho's fault.
                              Maybe I'm jealous
              I've given my reader no gaps
to leap across. My poems are
          a murder story, clear immediately that
                    someone will kill
                              someone else.

It's convention now
after the tragic event to say,   *There are no words.*
            But I believe there are always
words. There are, after all, bodies,
                        and they deserve words,
                            anybody's and mine.

            I am not saying close those brackets in Sappho,
crayon away
                the mystery of an unnamed love—
                            I am saying,
            Do not be satisfied
with our long pauses, if you can't hear
                        my heart, at least unstop your ears
for my profanities. Otherwise,
                            I find myself bloodless
as meat slabbed in a freezer, and these
                are bloody times.

        Reader,
let's not waste   our urgent and bright desires
                confessing what might have been. I want

        the ending we've earned,   not the sucker
                punch, but to stand
                                        with you
                in the path of the wallop.

II.

Nobody Wanted Such a River

Nobody needed it, nobody was curious about it.
—Mark Twain, *Life on the Mississippi*

Geography in 1608 being what it was,
Captain Smith thought he'd found
in the Chesapeake a way to the South Seas,
but the Susquehanna's narrow mouth
surprised his fleet after two miles, where
the plodding water turned rocky and rapid.
Go back, the Englishman might have said
to his crew. Or, staring into the faces
of chiefs who'd assembled at the banks,
Nothing here that matters, about the men

whose final grandsons would be scalped
two generations in by the Paxton Boys,
the Indians' war practice by then adopted
with European ferocity. I've peered through
the rail arches that line the Susquehanna,
poked the charcoaled embers of hobo camps.
I've watched fishermen throw back shad
corrupted by centuries of seeping mines,
and thought, I'm no different from anybody
else here, still shoving broken microwaves

into any sinkhole I can find. The river
runs acidic enough to pickle animals
and wafts like a latrine. But once,
when my ancestors first saw its waters,
trees muffled the forest floor to twilight
at noon. I'd like to live on the Susquehanna,
on that first farm, the only sound at night
a baby's murmuring, a child who'd grow

to produce its own babies. And so on, until
I imagine dozens of babies, over time,

in a house bricked before the Revolution,
as the towns built up around us took
for themselves some measure of stillness
that was ours. Every family corpse was buried
in the same lumpy field, and this will be
my end, too. So, despite the mine fire,
despite the changeless leach of the chemical
spill, despite trading our malignant
small-town hollow for the fetid trench
of the city, if I climb the blue mountain,

stand over its sweep of land and say, *Not me*,
I am lying. I was born fifteen minutes
up the Susquehanna from Three Mile Island
in the days they wondered if the check
for ruined DNA and bleeding orifices
was finally in the mail, where in the control room
one worker must've turned to another,
surrounded by incomprehensible machinery,
and wondered, *Did I do this?* But some errors
are too big to be the fault of one person,

and when I asked my mother why she and Dad
didn't flee with me, their new baby,
meltdown grave on every lip, she said,
Where were we supposed to go?
and I understood. Later, I used to cross the river
every day to buy Oxys in the section
of Harrisburg whose brick row houses
are shredded with flags, still in daylight
as a pocketed gun. We'd get in and get out,
crush the pills on books on the way home,

speeding by islands in a dry season,
or the rising sludge of an upriver rain.
My playground bordered tracks with great
screeching trains, and next to it, the river,
then the hill beyond where a troop of boy scouts
planted their half-assed flag. How could
I know about the approaching army of energy
companies, wells Roman in scale and ubiquity,
built to frack methane, light cities? Our
taps poisoned with champagne-colored

brack. Nothing to do about the wells,
so my brother tells me, when I offer to spark
the water from his faucet with my cigarette
lighter. Tapwater isn't a form of dignity
until it is. The river promises to swallow
tinkling pianos along with our garbage,
families grateful for any work,
each proposal for a dam or canal
promising a downward flow of money,
before the usual graft sets in. Twain said,

The Mississippi is in all ways remarkable,
but I've got nothing to say for this river.
It's like talking about my own blood,
trying to sense it shivering along
the walls of an artery. Billions
of gallons pass me by daily, and I never
see them again. But I am bound to them,
as a scalp to a skull. With our history,
second nature now to draw the knife
against our own crowns, and pull.

Livestock

When Neil Diamond played
the Farm Show in '66, somebody
shoved my mother, standing first
in the autograph line,
into him. She must have regretted
her broomhandle limbs,

flinching as her heel landed
hard on his foot, his response
the meanest thing a girl imagines
she'll hear from a man,
ever, in her lifetime: *Get this
fat girl offa me.* That's one version

of intimacy, a body invading
another's space, both recoiling
from trespass as if scalded.
For instance, my boyfriend
stopped sleeping with me
when I was fifteen. He said it felt
like a false kind of worship,

and I agreed, not because
we'd fashioned idols of each other,
as he thought, but he'd left me
unsure if my skin was still
on, or rubbed off
by his hands' dominion.
I've learned since then

to be the sour note in the cream's
churn, or condensation
on the nose of a farmer, carved

life-size from butter
and reefered behind glass
at the agricultural fair, so no one
can touch him. Now, walking
the Farm Show aisles among stolid,

bas relief cows, plain girls
cupping the heat of day-old chicks
to their chests, I've wondered
how they judge a pig without
cutting into it, goat
without the milk. The measure
turns out to be anatomy:

the level hip, foot alignment,
jigsaw of fat and muscle fibers
where every piece fits. We stand
outside the pen littered
with grassy shit and look
and look. But no matter
how perfect the form, we ask—
as if it can't be helped—
what the animal tastes like.

Tiniest of Shields

I hear my mother tell my nephew
what she once told me, in what
I know now is denial: *No one wants
to hurt you.* Then, the old owners
of our house left a merry-go-round
in the shed. No grand thing,

but a red bulb blazing atop two
rusted horses, their oily forelegs
raised in perpetual demonic charge.
The first time we invited other kids
over, my brother and I tried to show
it off. We pulled the lever that lurched

alive our toy, set the horses trotting
a circular shriek, friends begging us
to shut it down. You'd be surprised
how much violence a small town
can support—people were always
getting shot in town, or tied up,

tortured, and strangled. We ate
our ice cream at a parlor near
the duplex where the church's music
director, Mr. Halter, butchered
his family, then completed what papers
called "a bizarre quadrangle of death"

by piping carbon monoxide into
his car, Jesus songs he loved howling
on the tape deck. I tell my mother now
to teach the baby about fear at home—
because growing up, it seemed to me
every feral child reported on the news

was locked in my attic, my basement
the dirt floor where girl hostages
begged for their lives. Protected
at home from fear, I dragged it in
from town, wore it raw as a rabbit's
foot. When I looked at other children,

I'd see the metallic eggshell eyes
of the horses, and the shed's walls close,
flaking spiders. I want my nephew
prepared, when the lever is pulled,
for the engine that drives the hooves
forward, the horses seeing him.

Gifts

Some mornings at my office in Midtown,
post-9/11, shopping bags appeared
on my desk. In them, four-inch Louboutins,
a vintage bomber, Japanese stationary,
a Dior tote stuck with a Post-it, reading,
Toujours, Vincent. A buyer for Bendel's
in the '80s, he trolled couture auctions
when our boss was out. We sucked down
cigarettes on our breaks as flyover families,
eyes suctioned to the lenses of their
cameras, ambled among the drug fiends
scraping past on their daily haunt between
Penn Station and Port Authority.
We traded stories: his week lost to dope
in Paris for the morning I woke naked
on a rooftop ringed by butts and shards.
Marianne, Vincent called me. I was
the girl who swang from one Jagger clone
to the next, slim-hipped men who stepped
from doorways like rock stars deplane,
their bodies elegant and threatening
as the haunches of a horse. *Being young
is living outside of time*, Vincent said,
as we ate BLTs on the street, mayo
gumming the cracks of his oracular mouth.
Don't ever get old. I laughed, no idea
how it would one day feel, each year
peeling away a layer of girlish skin,
as I found fresh ways to sneer at dramas
my younger friends pined over,
You think that hurts? Today, years
from my last dance floor, I'd bathe
in virgin blood to stop feeling so wise.
Like my friend Vincent, I've got gifts now,

no one to give them to. He died early,
a heart attack in Harlem a year after
I'd moved out west, and no one
thought to pick up the phone. I had to
return to New York to hear it, and in
the spirit of *toujours*, to ask,
in this city towering with luxuries,
what thing could I possibly give someone?
If and when that friend arrives, let me
slip my present easily, sans ceremony,
over their bare shoulders.

D= R x T

At Portland International, at LaGuardia,
in the bathroom at Lambert, I'm forever
trying to snap on my garter belt and run toward
you, an umbra in glass at Charlotte Douglas,

hear the intercom voice suggest I *stay, see all*
[x] *city has to offer.* I've done turned-down beds
and rental cars, skymiles and customer rewards,
and now flying past the Arch, my seatmate asks,

What brings you to St. Louis? It's a test,
how long I'll live out of vending machines
on industrial highways for you, on sports bar
Manhattans marooned in their pools

of tepid ice, granola bars linted from a purse.
When I'm home, I recoil from my own lonely skin
between the sheets. But you're here in Arrivals,
keys jingling as you pick up my bag, as you did

five years ago, and you will five years from now.
Back home in a few days, I'll leave the luggage
zipped, my time with you archived, our sex
in short-term parking tucked into the seams

of an A-line skirt, or a sweater containing
the whole of the afternoon when you teach me
to ride a bike again, let me wipe my nose on
your sleeve in the park. Neither of us willing

to dampen the thrill of a friend you never grow
used to, the romantic weekends away that refuse
to sink into a home's worn upholstery. You and I
will end. I know this, as my limbs tumble

from the bike you've lent me, a squirrel bounding
sharply from my wheel. On my way home,
I'll scan Departures and consider picking one,
any point I can find on that urge for elsewhere—

Fort Lauderdale, Omaha, Anchorage, like a girl
I knew who took her car and drove, and too broke
for a hotel, parked behind a Yukon gas station,
engine and wipers on to whisk away the ice.

Andante Molto

I'd forgotten these violent winters, how snow
reels over the hills, polishing them to white glass,
not just reflecting, but shoving light back

at the sun. From the vantage of a train,
I peer into the ruddy postcards of kitchens,
people toweling dry dishes. In other houses,

people suit up to dig paths through
the snowdrifts. I hardly know the person
I've come for. She's dying, the woman

who bequeathed the blue carve of my eye sockets.
She knew me as a child, warmed beef stew
for me, bought the bike my parents wouldn't.

We didn't last much longer. Some friends
are better at five years old than thirty.
At her bedside, my hands clasp the rail,

like a ship's gunwale. I don't have my balance.
She offers the blunt triangle of a sandwich,
explains how they broke the news, told her

it was her time as if there were an order
of persons lined up for this great and stupid
march. I'd come with questions, want to pry

into her life like it's my property to inherit,
but then she asks, *How can someone suffer
this much and still live?* It's her way to describe

the valve calcified in her heart. Years ago
we watched *Peter and the Wolf,* French horns
swelling at the wolf's approach. Grandmother,

it would take years to mean all the things
we should say to each other now. Instead
we return to small talk, nothing words

for the snow to breathe into the tableaux
I'd seen stilled in my train window.
A stranger might love to hear them.

Temp

I brewed coffee for the salesmen at a dealership
by the airport, opening and closing cabinets
in canned air, wheeling my chair across the tiles,
my only job to smile at people who leaned
on reception and talked about their kids. The lady

I filled in for taped up a photo of her grandson,
a boy who watched me from the bulletin board.
I was eager to kill my time for six bucks an hour,
thought I saw his child's mouth say what kids
don't know: *It's not one choice but hundreds.*
When I stepped into the lot for a cigarette,
the sun lit every nerve, summer heat
smacking me back into my body. Despite
all the disappointed people I knew, I believed
the sky cupped down tight over median strips
and mini-malls would lift for me. But years later,

in another corporate office, a cubicle I leave
anonymous, sterile as the job I do there,
my days fall away like molted feathers. I think
the lady at the dealership must have retired
a while ago, with plastic stems of champagne
and store-bought cake. By now, she might
be dead. At night, my dreams are not subtle:
cannibals spreading sallow fat on biscuits,
the arms of undersea creatures waiting
to drag me down. And once, the boy

in the long-ago photo, who finishes what he had
to say to me: *You won't even feel it.* The next
day at my desk, the brittle force of my coughing
claps the office walls. No one asks how
I got here, or remembers whom I replaced.

PR Opportunity at the Food Bank

It's Thanksgiving and I'm at a dinner service
with a journalist, trying to wedge
my fable about urban generosity
into the newsroom's
mollusk heart. I stand next to mothers,
their kids shouting Christmas carols,
also day-laborers, ex-prisoners, someone's
grandmother, at one of the ministries
that feed people in the Bronx or Crown Heights
or Canarsie. I'm yanking people out of line

because I need stories, because the wallets
that open around Christmastime
have to know for whom. This interview
shouldn't be an interrogation,
but with the room's folding table and awful
light bulb, two white people,
me and a journalist, it's clear screws

will be put. I want to say to the person
in front of me, *I'm sorry I have to ask.* And because
no one needs a pass from me, I don't point out
the shame some feel their first time
taking charity. No shame

in lupus and HIV, the shit boyfriend,
the children who have moved on.
No talking about the mass of years carting home
jars of peanut butter and succotash. I ask

about things people are proud of:
their favorite foods to make, menudo or pecan pie;
a son doing well at math; what Haiti is like.

Ex-prisoners and present-day junkies say
they made mistakes, and I never ask what.
I can sell to a journalist
that the food pantry is another

bad break. In charity parlance, poor folks
are *just like us*, but say that here
to the scrawny child, to the armless man
a volunteer feeds peas by the spoonful. Tell it
to the home beautician's expert lace front.
Before we go in to our free lunch, I remind
the journalist to look people full in the face
before he takes their picture,

when food is offered, to accept and eat.
Instead his camera sticks to his glasses
like a brick wall. He picks at his plate
of Salisbury steak, and studying a woman
at our table, produces a question,
an American one—

Who's responsible for your poverty?

Honestly, I'm tired. I'd like to go home,
to my rosé, my couch, my nice neighborhood,
its plentiful Thai takeout and late shows
where comedians talk about something else.
I want to forget my sales pitch,
that this is how hunger ends, with chicken a la king
bubbling in Baptist kitchens, volunteers
who offer saran-wrapped dinner rolls along
with their prayers. But mostly,

I'd rewrite the journalist's story,
make it about the night the check clears,

how the scent of frying meat can bloom
through a hallway. About the gratitude of any
Friday, any old cinderblock,
the sheen of fat that rolls in the skillet,
children noisily free
of anyone's blessing. This is what I must picture
to do my job, not the scald
of chafing dishes in the priggish home

my journalist prefers, that Puritan
who can't locate the crumbs of his thanks
without a little help. I'll write for that person, too,
about the pleasure of a meal
without a poor neighbor's tribute
to soften under the tongue. A lead
so unlikely, it's news.

If You Are Confused About Whether a Girl Can Consent

... see if she can speak an entire sentence.
—Emily Doe

I find an earring in the bar
bathroom sink, last thing

I remember, then lose eight hours
in its drain. When I come to,

I'm hailing a cab. Sense gathers
in its backseat, tiny globes of water

condensing on a cold glass. I woke
sand-eyed, sprawled out

on the sidewalk, my limbs
barely beyond the heavy foot traffic

of an avenue. Who knows how many
stepped over or around me

to pass. Who taught me to brush
myself off and step toward

a cab's lights, give my address
in such even tones? Once home,

I check my skirt, no rips in it,
my workaday panties untorn

and practical as ever, my silence
bigger than this enormous gyre

of a city razed and rebuilt
each day by skyscraper

cranes. No bruises, no trace.
If I've been hurt, someone's put

the pieces back. Next morning,
I walk to work as usual,

the sidewalk whirling with receipts
and wrappers like snowflakes

made of garbage. Every party
has a fulcrum, everyone in control

and then no one. I look for one
clear moment to crowbar open,

recall an off-tune chord of laughter,
a baby face with a beard. Walking now,

my legs are dumb objects,
the space between elastic enough

to swallow all the men in New York,
or none of them, or one.

There's nothing I can report.
It's as though the night and its events

were projected on a screen behind me,
outside my field no matter

which way I turned. Like the plot
of a film you can't quite make out,

though you hear its gunshots
and screeching car tires from outside

the theater doors. Any sentence
I imagine I would have spoken

buried too far for the throat,
the lungs, the cunt, to reach.

On the Origin of Species

What if the pilled arms of waiting
room chairs in a fertility clinic
are the closest I come to natural selection,
date of my last period hard and fast
as my account balance, this perpetual

withdrawing of eggs? When I said
I wanted this—coughed out in some
exam room, *I want a baby*, as if
by saying it, someone else would
have to deal with that—the doctor

asked if I'd ever thought about
just having sex. As in, maybe
you find a decent man and forget
the condom, maybe you say
you're on the pill, and then

you do everything on your own,
like always. Instead I'm on Park Avenue
to see how many eggs I have left.
It turns out, a lot—grayscale caviar
on an ultrasound screen. But, soaking

in their nightly bath of wine,
I should be paid not to harvest them.
As if it could be entered on any chart
that in another life, while everybody
got lit in the other room, I'm the one

who cared for the dealer's toddler,
wiped up her spit, read to her from

a dingy picture book, as I waited for
my turn at the pipe. Because the binary
of women's choices is false, striver

or stroller maven, for years I played
the third option: sad sack who creeps
behind the yellow wallpaper of every
Can You Have It All? cover story, rank
with garlic and gin. I'm here now for

another chance, continuance. In this room
waiting with the others, all range
of middles belling outward, all order
of histories, I found my kind. Whatever else
we are, here to claim our children.

What Kind of Deal Are We Going to Make?

As a teenager, I found the remains of a fetus
in a plastic bag by the road. I wanted
to take it to the police, but my boyfriend
wouldn't let me put the bag in his car,
though every day I allowed him
to undress me in his parents' basement
in between rounds of World of Warcraft
and Doom, afternoons bursting the skulls
of his adversaries open with a semiautomatic.
It's dead, he said. *What are we supposed
to do about it?* We drove away. Of course
we did. What wouldn't I have traded then
for the balm of male affection, its
half-heart? Now I live on a bald scab
of grass, a swingset's chains twisting
figure eights, where I'll hide out until
I am the last woman standing. Once,
I followed a guy to a bar bathroom. Cutting
out lines on the counter, he said: *What kind
of deal are we going to make?* I pushed away
his hand heavy on my belly, his eyes
mugging my breasts. Running down
the hierarchy of flesh, he asked me to lift
my skirt, and I did, pulled it to the bloom
of my upper thigh. It's what a girl's days
are made of: What body part, this time?
And what will I get for it? I'm not sure
there's anything left of me, that palm-treed
oasis of okay I imagine for other people
always out of my reach. No inch
unclaimed, except I did what I thought
I wanted, and the reckoning that brought.

Takedown

The culture of sadism online has its own vocabulary and has gone mainstream.
—Jaron Lanier, *You Are Not a Gadget*

They say I did it all. No matter that I was home
binging on crime dramas, sad-drinking cans
of Coors. As ever it was, the best methodology
for devaluing a woman is to strap her body
to the cum-stained mattress of your mind. A nymph
at twenty-two, my pout and stare perfected

for the webcam, my lashes opened on an expanse
that could contain anything, my face a table
where others set their desires. At the millennium,
every cool girl styled an allegiance to corporate punk
by threading the same studded white belt through
her skinny jeans. We all practiced the same brand

of naive prurience, the saucy schoolgirl minted
in porn, deployed on rock-n-roll boys who
played and booked shows in Chinatown warehouses
and rooftop gardens, slept on floors when not
sleeping in vans. We girls were the first professionals
of the profile pic, guilded in Photoshop. Our rule

was to look anywhere but at the camera,
its lens masking the ether of strangers, guys
who just wanted *to bone*. So, I looked above,
or away, faking interest in a spiderweb, in a scarf
half-shed from its hook. From the digital woodwork
men thronged to me, boarded busses in lesser cities

for New York, to hold in their arms the girl
they'd clicked on, a girl who wasn't me, but someone

like me. It was the start of a new era of It Girls,
season of Chloë Sevigny, "discovered" by editors
in Washington Square hanging with skater kids,
Chloë of the cool so effortless it earned her

a *New Yorker* profile. On the messageboard,
we girls found admirers on virtual park benches.
Thrust into the amber honeycomb of modest fame,
few remembered the local queen deposed recently
to make room. Stunned by the glow of my new
digital identity, I touched my own face as if

for the first time. And while years later, I still don't
forgive him, I do understand the man who tried
to wreck my life, that dumpster-shaped rabbit
who'd been so clever online, ratcheting up snark
as a semi-legit film blogger. Nothing more vicious
than a nerd with a little power. At a bar one night,

I looked into his pink-edged avuncular eyes,
ignored the creep of his fingers on my waist,
and tried to be his friend. I didn't know rejection,
for some men, is a mother, and when she opens her legs,
she births monsters, three-headed, feathered with gills,
on a Hadean plain. So, he hacked my account,

texted other men pretending to be me, begged
on my behalf to blow them, sent photos
torrented from some troll-approved triple-X site
of someone else's tits, an engorged pussy that,
while beautiful, wasn't mine. This is how the other me
was born, stood up from her smut cradle, stretched

her limbs into the middle of a thousand fantasies.
I can no longer be surprised that so many men
stepped up to claim me—copped to fucking

the Whore of Babylon—because I've learned history
is a series of tents pitched by colonizers that plunder
the same land over and over, until the last garden

meets her toxic dawn as a dump. The shock
was the women, eager to act as support staff
to these jerks, the misogynist's version of interns.
Which is worse: a Brooklyn-based henhouse
of opportunists I never liked, gleefully diagnosing
my VD over disco fries, or my actual friends,

silent and spineless at the same checkered table?
On the Internet, I learned I'm down for threesomes,
wield the world's largest dildo, sell smack from
a cunt with a mighty case of herpes. I refused men
who thought I owed them, yet the best word for me
so many smart people could muster was *slut*.

And it's all still there—the takedown transcripted,
barbs never dulled when read a third or three-
hundredth time, when I give in and dig again
through the digital septic tank. Online assassination,
its insults perpetual, on hand for anyone to read
forever, would spur editorials and thinkpieces

long after I was told repeatedly, *Bitch, slit your wrists.*
Googling today, I can find that rabbitty shit
who once circulated "my" pussy photos. He's still
into movies, now famous for egging smallfry
in Tinseltown to off themselves, and for posting
footage on his blog of a girl being skullfucked,

cum dripping from her slack mouth. Some people
give themselves away so easily. This is what
some It Girls become, like me, a human zip file

of other people's malice. Meanwhile, the trolls
who once hassled me slid gently into their forties,
with mortgages, slipped discs, kids to tuck in.

I'd like to say I'm surprised to see they're still at it,
as drawn as ever to the tireless late-night thrill
of tapping out *dirty cunt*, tapping out *faggots*,
their lunch hours spent flushing new prey from
its quarry. On the same chats and comment boards,
I imagine a new generation logging in—

some that don't yet know the will of strangers
to seek and pierce their emotional centers,
and some to whom *kill yourself* will come easily,
like the echo of their fathers' voices. Soon enough,
the daughter I carry now will be there, too. I want
more for her than pussy shots and the vengeant

glow of an LED screen, a choice beyond
predator or prey. I'd give my daughter the power
to resist the inchoate purr of the It Girl
in her throat, the troll's easy welcome before
he takes her down. Refute any world, old or new,
that denies she is human. I'd say to her, *I'm here.*

Science Fiction: A Love Poem

My junkie best friend,
M., hoards sci-fi pulp mags,
files them in tubs in his basement.
On one of our good nights,
he digs up curling issues

of *Analog* and *Asimov's* for us to read
on his parents' porch, smoking
and searching for a favorite poem

about giant crabs attacking
Atlantic City. We're on fire
as only high people can burn.
In our subdivision, all the green
is curbed and contained, a handful

of gravel can be scooped up
and launched like a satellite, hurled
at the dew-stippled siding
of our parents' houses. But it's easier
to hit our veins, the beauty

and danger of them
yawning like plumeria
on the moon. I don't need to read

the story M. shares, I know the human
fear of Paleozoic consciousness
aimed at our destruction. I've read

scientists have proven
a crab feels pain when it's boiled—

shocked once, it retreats in its shell
at the signal of another. Only people
keep going back for more. Tonight,

painkillers wrap my skin in angora fur.
My mind, a knife in the velvet bag
of my body. M. is talking about
his favorite philosopher, Wittgenstein,
how he berated a colleague's wife

on a walk. She'd simply said,
What a beautiful tree, and he
started in, *what do you mean*

by "beautiful," what do you mean
by "tree." I listen from my slab
of concrete under the overdetermined

sky at the edge of our Northeast
megalopolis. I think our land
will be frontier again
someday, as the writers foretell,
when what we've built

falls down. M. puts a story in my hand,
in which the machine asks his creator
why evolved responses beat
coding *If A, then B*. But what if

there is no evolution,
beyond the good days
of the dope we share and its reliable
result? Other days we're mute,
pacing his garage, waiting for

an asshole dealer who never calls. Both
resigned to be the other's version
of love on offer, which is

a kind of score, but cut
with floor cleaner. If Wittgenstein
could see us, he'd say there is no
ordinary language for what we are,
nothing to tie us

to this manifold of planets
stamped in the pulp we read. Sci-fi
requires the rules of any given

universe follow logic, like rules
on Earth. No world will
recognize us otherwise.

What Is the Sisterhood to Me?

Do you know yourself? I thought I did
at nineteen, when my boyfriend called
from the hospital to say he'd been hit
in the face with a fire extinguisher
and got kicked out of school *because
of some dumb bitch.* And so I drove

to Westchester General that night,
four hours, to see how bad it was,
the muscles he used to grimace
barely refit to his facial bones,
his nostrils plugged with rust-colored
gauze. Maybe I already knew a girl
hit him, not a coked-out buddy
or a crew from Yonkers, but I needed
to hear, in person, why a woman
would try to split the bridge
of a man's nose like the seam
on a baseball. My boyfriend knew

what so many men know: if you don't
admit it, it's not true. That in a year
I would still bake cookies for him,
wrapping them in a coffee can bound
for his boot camp at Fort Jackson.
He'd never tell me who hit him.
But I'd see her in the faces
of other women at college, where
we spun pots and talked about Plath,
avoiding the story they all knew,
that I was the one whose boyfriend
tried to rape a woman.
I didn't know what I was capable of

at thirteen, when the softball captain
cornered me in the bathroom, held
my face in her hands and spat in it,
sneering, *Why don't you talk?* Or when
my father told me in the car one day
he didn't believe I'd ever get married.
But I was determined, the stringy
teenager who picked out

"Stand by Your Man" on the guitar.
I fucking *got* that song, its notes already
chording in me, like the woman
who lives, as Adrienne said,
in the queasy strobe light
of the lie. Don't say you know yourself
unless you've stepped outside of it,
seen the shadow you cast
in your own bronze light.

Take me, for instance—
I never would have guessed,
holding the fire extinguisher,
how nearly weightless it is
in my woman's hands.

Recalibration

Sometimes one person is the gravitational center
of shit going wrong. One time, I was at a bodega
in Brooklyn, scanning the beer cooler,
when townies kicked over a tower of soup cans,
cylinders of chicken rice and minestrone
pelting the stockboy. Their challenge:
Pick it up, Habib, where are your
seventy-two virgins now? The boy was Arab,
aware as anyone else of our new, still-smoldering
skyline, the malt liquor bottles on the shelves
lined up as precisely as a soldier's salute,

and he saw the target I became
when instinctually I turned
toward our midnight shift of berserkers,
said, *Do you really have to do this?* In that moment,
his problem became mine,
the gameshow wheel of categorical abuses
sailing past its black people and queer boys,
past its recent immigrants, the needle finally landing
on me, a woman, just one more
kind of other. Though sometimes

I escape it. Like a few months earlier,
when during the Republican Convention,
I dully circled Madison Square Garden
as if it were an object I couldn't find. Then
the cops told us, schoolteachers and civil servants,
political weekenders at best, without a permit
we could only march single file. So we sang
"This Land is Your Land" straight up the steel cleft
of Broadway for fifty well-mannered blocks,
until the line buckled and police nets
unfurled. I heard, then, the lead officer point me out,

cheap suit I wore for the journalists, as he told
his riot squad to arrest everyone
but me. And another cop, hissing, through his helmet:
Sweetheart, you'll have to do something
really illegal. Hard to make a point
wearing the face of every

white cop's daughter. And while technically
not illegal, this is why I mouthed off
at the creeps who decided to stalk me down
the long, unlit path between the bodega
and home, an avenue usually flush
with flower peddlers, moms with strollers,
hobos and their carts, but this was Sunday night,
two a.m., and I was considering how fast
I could actually run. I was considering
the next lit storefront, the safety of eyes inside,
when the men took a shot: *Fat bitch!*
I'll fuck you hard enough to kill you! So I ran—
to the best hiding place I could reach, the alley
behind the church, St. Anthony's, and crouched

in the shadow of a storage box, clutching
a bottle of malt liquor like a weapon,
I don't know for how long,
as the men, still searching, passed me by.

***

I'll leave myself there.
I'll let you imagine how I got home that night,
though I'll say I kept thinking about the boy
restacking his soup cans in the yellow glow
of the bodega, but I never went back. I'd turned,
as if by reflex, to help him, watched his darting eyes

settle with relief. And we'd both seen,
unmistakable, the shadow of the men's rage
shifting, heard the *cha-chunk* as the crosshairs
found my body. And I'll ask you,
ten years later, what does it mean

that I felt foolish? More often than I'll admit,
I pass by an instance where I know
I should stop—a circle of cop cars, or a huddle
of boys, at their center, like open-air flesh
in an operating theater, a figure I can
hardly see, outnumbered, afraid,
yet resolved to accept the punishment no one earns—
and I go on past,
and though I sometimes circle back, by then,
of course, by then,
whoever it was is gone.

Jersey Valentine

Chowder houses shut, skeeball
arcades silent, their bowls of bisque

and prize counters picked clean, I drive
south to an off-season shore town,

bundled up, with a cooler of wine
that is pink and too sweet. The wind

blows loud down the white beach,
up to an empty house where someone

could congratulate herself on
being alone, until the lights shudder

and the garbage disposal
turns over. *A ghost*, my brother says

when I call him, tell him I woke
to a beam of refrigerator light

shining across the carpet. I'm calm.
One by one, I rehang the towels

that leap from their racks.
But when I find a wreath of stems

laid out on the bathroom tile like
a wet mouth, I bolt to the nearest bar

just before closing, no coat
and snow in my hair, and tell a boy

from Kansas City in a rumpled shirt
I'm afraid to go home. He smiles,

You can stay with me, and I'm about
to do it, I want the human, the living,

until I tune myself again to the signals
of a ghost: what I'd found on the floor

was a bouquet, a gift. A ghost
chose me. Returning, I walk back

in the sleet, peering in moonlight
at the lived-in houses, stilled in the way

people left them, living people
I'll never meet. At home, I arrange

my bouquet of stems, the appliances
blinking goodnight. As I sleep, I allow

a cold breath to graze my neck.
Oh, it whispers. *You must be the wind.*

Correspondence Theory

In Winn-Dixie, where I've never seen
anyone buy flowers, a box of rose petals
has been sweating inside a tiny refrigerator

all Valentine's week. I can't help but
consider who would buy them, the unlikely
art of their hands as they pullstrip

open the container to scatter petals
like rubber lips on the bed, on the table
before the romantic meal. I'm here with a basket

of ingredients for a hamburger bean pie
you'll eat in silence. I saw an accident
on the way, was listening to the traffic report

as the car in front of me swung into
the opposing lane. I saw it coming,
but couldn't stop the car's body erupting

as if discharged from inside. Then quiet,
a still figure, indistinctly human. I've been
inside that car, been that figure, asking:

*Is it broken? Is this my blood? Are these
my hands moving?* I mistrusted
my perspective. Now I know the inside

and outside of an accident are the same.
I count the romantic gestures completed
on my behalf on one hand, in the wine aisle.

I know we are not cars. But I wonder
if your other woman appreciates
the dulcet stink of your ear canal, like oil

on a switchblade. I read the covers
of the women's magazines, drink in
their exuberant defeat. I, too, know

how thin one can slice a word and still
have enough to live. This is how it tastes,
like sucking a dirty half-dollar, like

emerging from the car, as a radio announcer
reports what feels like my accident in
real time. He suggests another route to take.

With Gratitude to Those Who Have Made This Book Possible

With the rich and mighty, always a little patience.
—"Spanish proverb" in *The Philadelphia Story*

I've got a story for you where I'm the asshole,
and the other assholes in it are my friends. A story
about the lives most of us will never afford,
though their scuttlebutt details seduce us. Its subject
is the people, and the parts of the city, that turn

the majority of us into Victorian urchins,
noses pressed against steamy bakery windows.
Among these friends is my college roommate,
who every summer invites me to her French chalet,
routinely forgetting that in order to eat

I heave my body daily into a Midtown office.
She tells me I'm better than that job when I decline.
But today I've been asked to a Prospect Park picnic,
and when I arrive, I'm hugged earnestly, invited
to sample citrus oil from someone's endless

cache of gift bags. I've brought a summer salad,
corn and heirloom tomatoes from the greenmarket
I diced carefully to impress people that I'd hoped
a decade ago to be like, girls whose fathers built
pipelines in Africa while they wrote papers

about French Colonialism in school. Back then,
I pretended to be them, though at night I joined
the other scholarship kids to prank numbers
from our school directory, roused gentle Bitsy
from Potomac or dyspeptic Mortimer in Bel Air

at three a.m., because I could. Every distant
family member of mine would have to die at once
to inherit me into one of my friends' second homes.
Of course I felt inadequate. But we spent
so much time together, it seemed I'd as easily

marry a Belgian prince or a hedge fund wunderkind
as they would. That first summer after college,
walking in Strawberry Fields, my dad asked me
why I didn't rent one of those little attics
on Central Park West. He was unable to fathom

the duplex penthouse behind dainty windows,
or that at sleepovers at ones like it, I hesitated
to spit my toothpaste in Italian marble sinks.
And now my friends can't picnic in Brooklyn
without someone commenting on the park's

illusion of equality. Nearby, ordinary people
are frying their plantains, circling the clumpy field
in a game of pick-up soccer. From their vantage
I am the rich person, coddled as a tiny duke
or duchess in a Renaissance court painting,

or at least one of the glossy mastiffs they liked
to pose alongside. I only exist by proximity.
But it's proximity that grants me a peek
into the bespoke panic room that generates
so much of what we call art and who gets

to make art. The fault of these friends I look
at the acknowledgments of certain books
and find I've been the plus one at birthdays
for Brooklyn literati, people whose patios
reminded me of the time needed to write a book,

how the sting of rejection might be reduced
on a golden cloud. Of course I was dying to go.
I've got a talent for noticing these friends'
failures, their bakery scones staling in the sun,
not an oily kernel left of my corn salad. My job

is to notice. I imagine the architects who sculpted
the park's hills, believing the poor deserved
their share of countryside, and how growing up,
I bit into tomatoes we grew ourselves. We made
our own pleasures, unprofitable as the hue

on a piece of fruit. Vendors push the day's last
coconut ices, as the sun sets on a lawn strewn
with chicken bones, soccer balls flattened to discs.
They have been kicked so hard, and so often.
How recently they amused somebody.

The Valkyrie

Strapped to the wheel of perpetual
awareness, I listen as my boss says, if I want
to keep my job, I'd best think hard, not about

the minutes I waste, but the seconds. So when
a man catches the ATM door behind me,
each blink I take feels like a good, long

sleep I've earned. I don't notice, at first,
the worm of his moustache, butter-colored
arms starred with moles, or the side-pocket

protrusion of his gun until he motions
at it, then me, to hand him the single crisp bill
I've withdrawn to help me get hammered

tonight. It's already growing soft as I wad it
into his palm, relieved to comply completely,
to be sure of doing it right. But then he says,

Take out the rest. Now, with the barrel nudging
my left lung, there it is on the screen,
in the certainty of 1s and 0s, how little

I have left. Only last night, I went home
with a guy who asked me to strangle him,
so I put my hands on his neck and squeezed,

said, *No one will even notice you're gone*
in the stony voice I usually reserve for myself.
The words came easily, but how loud they were

in that musk-hot room, how his body tensed
felt new. So I move to snatch back the bill,
and my robber's hand opens as if he expects it,

the rule that anything given in the world is soon
retracted. The gun there, still. And me,
banking on him as the kind to shove a girl

down a flight of stairs, that they'll do enough
work to shut her up. But there are no stairs,
no hypothetical falls, just my explanation

to him that today I turned off the lights
in the supply closet to cry. How pieces of me
remain in my office cube long after security

sets the night alarm, and that some part
of me is always there, two eyes under a desk—
the same hapless Valkyrie hitching up my skirt

each morning to ride into Port Authority,
drawing against the water torture of a system
that owns my sword, portions out my rations,

and his. His hard face breaks into pity, eyes
and jaw relaxing. He puts the gun away,
a teenager in dirty jeans, skin of the innocent,

and says, *Don't tell anyone. Please.* My eyes
close against the war drum of our twinned
pulses. The wheel stops for us. It finally stops.

Notes

The telephone dialogue in "The Lovely Voice of Samantha West" is lifted from a 2013 article by Denver Nicks in *Time* magazine ("Robot Telemarketer Employer: Samantha West Is No Robot").

"The Evacuation Shadow" references a human behavior phenomenon, the evacuation shadow effect, in which far more residents will voluntarily leave the area surrounding a nuclear power plant following an accident than government officials advise or plan.

Much of the Pennsylvania history in "Nobody Wanted Such a River" is based on research compiled in *Susquehanna, River of Dreams* by Susan Q. Stranahan (Johns Hopkins University Press, 1995).

"Tiniest of Shields" references the Halter family murder-suicide that took place in Duncannon, Pennsylvania, in 1965. As it was 1965, there were no Jesus songs *on the tape deck*, but Byron Halter held a prominent place in the church and town.

The title of "If You Are Confused About Whether a Girl Can Consent" is from the published testimony of Emily Doe in the Brock Turner rape case. The full sentence is: "Future reference, if you are confused about whether a girl can consent, see if she can speak an entire sentence."

The messageboard in "Takedown" is (was) makeoutclub.com.

The short story referenced in "Science Fiction: A Love Poem" is "Silently and Very Fast" by Catherynne M. Valente.

"What Is the Sisterhood to Me?" is indebted to Adrienne Rich, not least for the line "lives in the queasy strobe light of the lie," taken in modified form from "The Lie of Compulsory Female Heterosexuality."

Acknowledgments

Grateful acknowledgment is made to the following journals in which poems in this collection have previously appeared, some in slightly different versions or with different titles:

Alaska Quarterly Review: "Nobody Wanted Such a River"; *The Awl*: "The Valkyrie"; *Bennington Review*: "Tiniest of Shields"; *Crab Orchard Review*: "Girls"; *Gargoyle*: "On the Origin of Species"; *Green Mountains Review*: "Gifts" and "If You Are Confused About Whether a Girl Can Consent"; *Grist Poetry Journal*: "Conversion Party"; *LIT*: "The Lovely Voice of Samantha West"; *Narrative*: "Anticonfessional"; *The Nassau Review*: "Barrier Islands"; *The Pinch*: "Reading Sappho's Fragments"; *Pleiades*: "Science Fiction: A Love Poem"; *Prairie Schooner*: "What Is the Sisterhood to Me?"; *Queen Mob's Tea House*: "Takedown"; *Scoundrel Time*: "PR Opportunity at the Food Bank" and "With Gratitude to Those Who Have Made This Book Possible"; *Spry Literary Journal*: "Temp"; *Sugar House Review*: "The Evacuation Shadow" and "Livestock"; *Tampa Review*: "What Kind of Deal Are We Going to Make?"

"Girls" appeared in *The Best American Poetry 2016*, and "On the Origin of Species" appeared in *Best New Poets 2013*.

Many thanks to the friends, family, teachers, and colleagues who have supported my life in poetry: Marcus Cafagña, Selby M. Doughty, George and Cheryl Hoover, Matthew Hardin, Tracie Morris, Soledad Fox, Garrett Hongo, Dorianne Laux, Paul Martone, Hilary Baldwin, Andrew Epstein, Keith Kopka, Maari Carter, Cate Marvin, James Kimbrell, Daisy Fried, Mark Bibbins, Sandra Simonds, and Lee Folmar.

Special thanks to the readers and editors who have pulled my work from various slush piles, especially Brenda Shaughnessy, Allison Joseph, Edward Hirsch, Dana Levin, Dana Curtis, and Kathryn Nuernberger.

My deepest gratitude to Erin Belieu, whose kind and insightful suggestions resulted in this version of the book.

TITLES FROM ELIXIR PRESS

POETRY

Circassian Girl by Michelle Mitchell-Foust

Imago Mundi by Michelle Mitchell-Foust

Distance From Birth by Tracy Philpot

Original White Animals by Tracy Philpot

Flow Blue by Sarah Kennedy

A Witch's Dictionary by Sarah Kennedy

The Gold Thread by Sarah Kennedy

Rapture by Sarah Kennedy

Monster Zero by Jay Snodgrass

Drag by Duriel E. Harris

Running the Voodoo Down by Jim McGarrah

Assignation at Vanishing Point by Jane Satterfield

Her Familiars by Jane Satterfield

The Jewish Fake Book by Sima Rabinowitz

Recital by Samn Stockwell

Murder Ballads by Jake Adam York

Floating Girl (Angel of War) by Robert Randolph

Puritan Spectacle by Robert Strong

X-testaments by Karen Zealand

Keeping the Tigers Behind Us by Glenn J. Freeman

Bonneville by Jenny Mueller

State Park by Jenny Mueller

Cities of Flesh and the Dead by Diann Blakely

Green Ink Wings by Sherre Myers

Orange Reminds You Of Listening by Kristin Abraham

In What I Have Done & What I Have Failed To Do by Joseph P. Wood

Bray by Paul Gibbons

The Halo Rule by Teresa Leo

Perpetual Care by Katie Cappello

The Raindrop's Gospel: The Trials of St. Jerome and St. Paula by Maurya Simon

Prelude to Air from Water by Sandy Florian

Let Me Open You A Swan by Deborah Bogen

Cargo by Kristin Kelly

Spit by Esther Lee

Rag & Bone by Kathryn Nuernberger

Kingdom of Throat-stuck Luck by George Kalamaras

Mormon Boy by Seth Brady Tucker

Nostalgia for the Criminal Past by Kathleen Winter

Little Oblivion by Susan Allspaw

Quelled Communiqués by Chloe Joan Lopez

Stupor by David Ray Vance

Curio by John A. Nieves

The Rub by Ariana-Sophia Kartsonis

Visiting Indira Gandhi's Palmist by Kirun Kapur

Freaked by Liz Robbins

Looming by Jennifer Franklin

Flammable Matter by Jacob Victorine

Prayer Book of the Anxious by Josephine Yu

flicker by Lisa Bickmore

Sure Extinction by John Estes

Selected Proverbs by Michael Cryer

Rise and Fall of the Lesser Sun Gods by Bruce Bond

I will not kick my friends by Kathleen Winter

Barnburner by Erin Hoover

FICTION

How Things Break by Kerala Goodkin

Juju by Judy Moffat

Grass by Sean Aden Lovelace

Hymn of Ash by George Looney

Nine Ten Again by Phil Condon

Memory Sickness by Phong Nguyen

Troglodyte by Tracy DeBrincat

The Loss of All Lost Things by Amina Gautier

The Killer's Dog by Gary Fincke

Everyone Was There by Anthony Varallo

The Wolf Tone by Christy Stillwell